BELLS AND BELLRINGING

John Harrison

SHIRE PUBLICATIONS
Bloomsbury Publishing Plc

Kemp House, Chawley Park, Oxford OX2 9PH, UK
29 Earlsfort Terrace, Dublin 2, Ireland
1385 Broadway, 5th Flr, New York, NY 10018, USA
Email: shire@bloomsbury.com
www.shirebooks.co.uk

SHIRE is a trademark of Osprey Publishing Ltd

First published in Great Britain in 2016
Transferred to digital print in 2022

Shire Library no. 802
Print ISBN: 978 0 74781 433 7
ePDF: 978 1 78442 090 1
ePub: 978 1 78442 089 5

Typeset in Garamond Pro and Gill Sans
Printed and bound in India by Replika Press
Private Ltd.

23 24 25 26 27   10 9 8 7 6 5

The Woodland Trust
Shire Publications supports the Woodland Trust, the
UK's leading woodland conservation charity.

www.shirebooks.co.uk
To find out more about our authors and books visit
our website. Here you will find extracts, author
interviews, details of forthcoming events and the
option to sign-up for our newsletter.

COVER IMAGE
Cover design by Peter Ashley. Front cover: Bell sallies
at St Michael's, Steventon, Oxfordshire (photograph
by Nick Wright).

TITLE PAGE IMAGE
Overhead view of a weekly ringing practice at
All Saints, Wokingham.

CONTENTS PAGE IMAGE
The masthead of *The Ringing World*, the ringing
community's weekly newspaper, which has been
providing news, views and information about bells,
ringers and ringing since 1911, and is the journal of
record for performances.

ACKNOWLEDGEMENTS
I owe a debt to the many ringing historians on whose
work I have drawn for this book. I would particularly
like to thank Chris Pickford whose help and guidance
has proved invaluable. Thank you too to the many
fellow ringers and others who have so generously
allowed me to use their pictures. Finally, thanks to
my wife Anne for proofreading the book and to
Helen Craig for reading it from the perspective of
non-ringing readers for whom it is mainly written.
Any remaining defects are of course mine.

Images are acknowledged as follows:

I would like to thank the following for permission
for me to use their pictures:

David Beacham, page 21; Anthony Bianco, page
50; Kurt Brown, page 54; Russell Butcher, page 11
(bottom); Central Council of Church Bell Ringers,
pages 6 (top), 56; Charmborough Trust, page 55
(right); Christopher Dalton, pages 20, 23 (right);
Duncan Davies, page 55 (left); Philip Earis/David
Pipe, page 51 (bottom); Anne Frith/Nony Olerenshaw,
page 38 (right); Sean Gallup (Getty images), page 57;
Alan Glover, page 27; Frank King, page 29; Frank
Lewis, page 40 (right); Dickon Love, page 24; Len
Morris, page 44; Richard Nicholls, page 47; Sylvia
& Michael Porter, page 38 (left); The Ringing World,
page 3; Trisha Shannon, page 16; Robert Smith, page
51 (top); Mark Strupczewski, page 11 (top); John
Sutton, page 34; Taylor Bells, page 53; Neil Thomas,
pages 4, 28; Peter Titmuss (Alamy Stock Photo),
page 32; Mike Toze, page 43; Michael Wilby, page
49 (bottom); Wikimedia Commons, pages 12, 37,
40 (left). All other pictures are from the author's
collection or are in the public domain.

CONTENTS

BELLS AND BELL-HANGING

Bells are the loudest of musical instruments. They are capable of arousing strong emotions and their sound is deeply rooted in many cultures around the world. In England and some other parts of the English-speaking world the unique sound of English-style ringing, especially change ringing, is embedded in the public consciousness. The bells do not 'play tunes', nor do they strike randomly as they do in many places. They sound in ordered sequences, which continually change to create a captivating soundscape. This unique style of ringing is made possible by the special way the bells are hung, so let us start by looking at 'how' ringing works.

FULL-CIRCLE RINGING
Bells can be fixed mouth down and struck by a hammer or clapper as they are in clocks and carillons (where the clappers are operated from a clavier), or they can be 'chimed' (swung through a small arc with the clapper swinging inside the bell), but English-style ringing is much more dynamic with the bells swinging full circle – mouth up to mouth up. The clapper strikes the bell hard at the end of each swing, alternately on each side. Ringing in this way means that the timing can be controlled very accurately. When the bell is swinging nearly full circle, making it swing a little higher makes it swing more slowly and letting it swing less high makes it swing more quickly. This is what makes it easy to ring bells in orderly sequences, and to vary the order continually – the essence of change ringing.

The bells of St Magnus the Martyr, London, viewed from above.

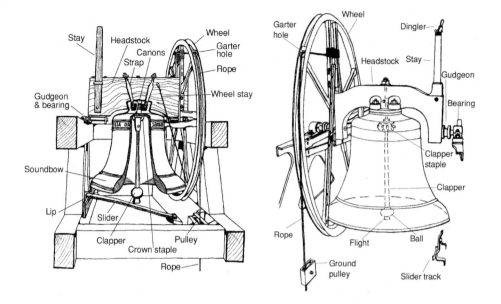

Fig. 1: Bells hung for full-circle ringing with typical fittings: traditional timber headstock (left); modern metal headstock (right).

Each bell is mounted on a headstock with bearings so that it can turn freely. A wheel is attached to the headstock and around it passes the rope that runs down to the ringing room below. Also on the headstock is a stay that allows the bell to rest mouth up just beyond the balance point when it is not being rung.

In English-style ringing the rope is the ringer's only contact with the bell apart from hearing it. The ringer feels what the bell is doing and judges how far to let the rope rise, and when and how much force to apply to make the bell strike at the

Fig. 2: The position of bell, clapper, stay, slider and rope when the bell is up – set at handstroke (left) and set at backstroke (right) – compared with when the bell is down (centre).

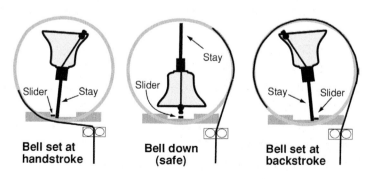

right time. The rope winds in opposite ways around the wheel at each end of the swing ('backstroke' and 'handstroke'). The rope includes a tufted woollen portion, the 'sally', for the ringer to grip when not holding the tail end (see *Fig. 3*).

Once a bell is swinging full circle it takes relatively little effort to sustain it. Typical bells weigh between a quarter and three-quarters of a ton – some lighter, some much heavier. The number of bells in a ring can vary. Each has a different note in a diatonic scale, with the bells generally getting heavier down the scale and with the ropes falling more or less in a circle, in order. Over five hundred towers have a ringing bell heavier than a ton, with the heaviest (over four tons) at Liverpool Anglican Cathedral. Ringing on heavier rings of bells is generally slower because they naturally turn more slowly.

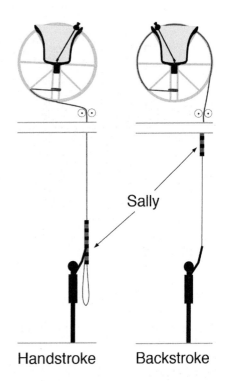

Sally

Handstroke   Backstroke

Fig. 3: The rope wraps a long way over the wheel at backstroke and a short way under the wheel at handstroke, so the ringer holds the rope end at backstroke but at handstroke holds the sally with the spare rope hanging below the hands.

Raising a bell from the safe mouth-down position to the 'up' position ready for ringing takes significant effort to swing it progressively higher until it is swinging full circle and ready to be 'set' (rested against the stay). Heavy bells take longer and may need more than one person to do this. Such bells are often left up rather than being lowered between sessions.

MAKING BELLS

The Chinese were casting metal bells around 2000 BC but they varied in shape, without the lip of modern bells. Early metal bells in Europe were made by bending a sheet of metal into a shape like a cow bell, but by the fourth or fifth century large bells were being cast. Molten bronze at about 870°C was (and still is) poured into moulds made for each specific bell.

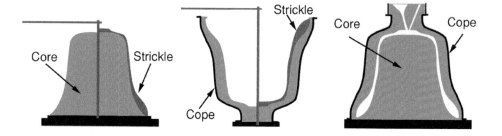

Fig. 4: Three stages in making a bell mould: forming the core; forming the outer; the completed mould.

Casting a bell. At the Whitechapel Bell Foundry the founder supervises the pouring of molten metal from the crucible into the mould.

Historically bells were cast using the lost-wax process in which a solid mould surrounds a wax model of the bell that is then melted out to leave a bell-shaped cavity. The method now used for casting British bells, where the cavity is formed without a wax model, dates from the mid nineteenth century. A core is built of brick on a metal base plate and covered with loam (a mixture of sand, clay, straw, horse manure and animal hair). The outer shape is then built inside a large iron casing called a cope, also using loam. The fibrous content binds the loam together and burns away to create microscopic tubes for air to escape when the metal is poured in.

The profiles of both parts are accurately formed using a strickle – a board shaped like the profile of the bell to be cast, which is rotated around the mould to create the circular profile. The loam is gradually built up by hand, with the strickle skimming off any excess or showing where more is needed.

The moulds are dried in an oven and coated with graphite to give a high finish. The inscriptions and decoration are formed by pressing appropriate letters and patterns into the inside of the outer

mould before final drying. This forms a raised pattern on the bell when cast.

The two parts are aligned and clamped together to form a cavity the size and shape of the bell, with vents and a basin to pour in the metal. Large moulds are buried in a pit to take the weight of the metal and ensure even cooling, which takes several days. After cooling the moulds are broken away to release the bells. The metal copes and baseplates can be reused but the actual moulds have to be discarded.

Bronze, an alloy of 77 per cent copper and 23 per cent tin, is an ideal material to use. Harder and more elastic than either metal alone, it is resonant enough to vibrate with a strong clear sound when struck but also tough enough not to break from continual pounding by the clapper.

A bell vibrates in many different ways at once, and the sound contains many different 'partial frequencies'. Over the centuries founders evolved the shape and thickness of bells by trial and error to produce an acceptable sound but the result could be unpredictable – some bells didn't have quite the intended note and some had a poor tone. The founder could alter a bell's note a little by 'chip tuning', removing pieces of metal from inside the bell mouth with a pointed hammer. Bells that didn't need chip tuning were 'maiden bells'. Little could be done to improve a bell with poor tone other than melting it down and replacing it.

Modern bells are tuned on a vertical lathe by selectively removing metal from the inside. A skilled tuner can judge the

Oak leaves and acorns around the inscription band of the tenor bell at Wokingham (also known as Oakingham in the eighteenth century), made in 1703 by Samuel Knight.

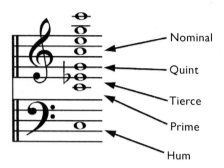

Nominal

Quint

Tierce

Prime

Hum

Above: *Fig. 5:* The partial tones of a bell in C, showing the five that are tuned in true harmonic tuning.

Above right: Evidence of earlier chip tuning (crude vertical ridges above) as well as cuts by a modern tuning lathe (fine horizontal cuts below).

Opposite: Historic bells on display in the cloisters at Worcester Cathedral.

right amount to remove from the right places to achieve the desired effect. Bells in a ring are tuned to sound the correct note relative to each other as well as having the five main partial frequencies of each individual bell (named in *Fig. 5*) brought into a harmonic relationship. This 'true harmonic tuning' gives a rich tone.

Bells by UK founders prior to the late nineteenth or early twentieth century varied a lot in their tuning. The term 'old style' tuning is often used for such bells that differ significantly from true harmonic tuning, but it is an imprecise term and there is considerable variation even between bells of the same founder. Thus, while some 'old style' bells produce an agreeable sound, others do not, and there is quite a bit of subjectivity.

Bells don't go out of tune but if they were cast with poor tone or not quite the right note they can sometimes be improved using modern techniques. Retuning a bell selectively removes small amounts of metal from different parts of the bell to alter the strike note or some of the partials.

CONSERVATION

Bells are inherently long-lasting and a few survive from the twelfth and thirteenth centuries. Most are more recent, either installed as part of newer installations or as replacements for older bells. Over the centuries bells have been replaced for many reasons. Some were lost in accidents or fires and some were cracked. Many were considered of poor quality, or contemporary tastes changed. In 2014 about 6 per cent of extant bells dated from before 1600, 31 per cent from between 1600 and 1800, 27 per cent from between 1800 and 1900, and 36 per cent from after 1900.

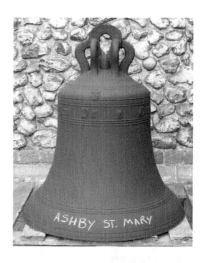

When bells in a ring are replaced the new bells are generally described as 'recast', with the inscriptions of the old bells often copied on to the new ones along with details of the new casting. In the past replaced bells were often melted down but in modern times more effort is made to find new uses for surplus bells that are in good condition. Using some second-hand bells can help make an installation affordable that would not otherwise be. The supplier also receives a better price than for scrap metal, and the bell is kept in use rather than being lost. Between 1992 and 2014 the Keltek Trust helped to rehome some 650 bells.

A medieval bell from Ashby St Mary, Norfolk, after a large crack was repaired by welding.

In 1967 successful research at the Welding Institute sponsored by the Council for the Care of Churches and the Worshipful Company of Founders led to the foundation in 1968 of Soundweld, a company specialising in welding cracked or broken bells. By 2014 this organisation had repaired some 800 bells, around a third of which were historic or listed bells that have thus been conserved for continued use. Historic bells that are no longer used are sometimes retained for public display.

TINTINNALOGIA:
OR,
THE ART
OF
RINGING.
WHEREIN

Is laid down plain and easie Rules for Ringing all forts of *Plain Changes*.

Together with

Directions for Pricking and

Ringing all *Cross Peals* ; with a full Difcovery of the Myftery and Grounds of each Peal.

AS ALSO

Inftructions for *Hanging of Bells,* with all things belonging thereunto.

By a Lover of that ART.

A. Perfii Sat. v.
Difce : fed ira cadat nafo, rugofaque fanna,

LONDON,

Printed by *W. G.* for *Fabian Stedman,* at his fhop in St. *Dunftans* Church-yard in *Fleetftreet.* 1668.

CHANGE RINGING

THIS CHAPTER GIVES a very brief overview of the richness and complexity that emerged from the seemingly simple desire to ring different sequences in a systematic way. The first thing to realise is that, although change ringing is a form of music, and a ring of bells is tuned to a musical scale, ringing is not described with musical notation but with numbers. Each bell is numbered down the scale, starting with 1, regardless of the key to which the bells are tuned. The bells sound in successive 'rows', in each of which every bell strikes once. Ringing normally starts with 'rounds', ringing down the scale. On six bells this is 123456, on eight bells 12345678, and so on.

A bell takes about two seconds to swing and, because the timing can only be varied a little, it imposes a constraint that no bell ever moves more than one place between successive rows. 123456 can be followed by 124356, and 142356 could follow that. But 142356 cannot directly follow 123456 because bell 4 would have to move two places at once, between 4th and 2nd. The movement between one row and the next is called a 'change' (though confusingly many people also call rows 'changes').

Opposite: The title page of *Tintinnalogia*, the first book on change ringing, published in 1668.

Fig. 6: Some musical rows in ringing notation and musical notation (assuming a key of C), showing the patterns that make them attractive to the ear.

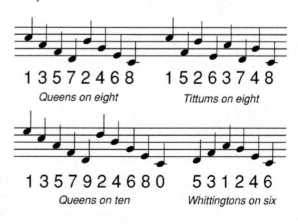

1 3 5 7 2 4 6 8
Queens on eight

1 5 2 6 3 7 4 8
Tittums on eight

1 3 5 7 9 2 4 6 8 0
Queens on ten

5 3 1 2 4 6
Whittingtons on six

Opposite: *Fig. 8:*
Plain Bob Minor
showing the
path of a bell
through the
course, which
can be learnt as
a pattern.

In each change one or more pairs of adjacent bells swap places. That constraint underlies the unique character of change ringing. It might sound very limiting, but the combinatorial nature of changes gives huge scope for variety in performances.

The simplest form of change ringing is 'call changes' where the conductor periodically calls a pair of bells to swap places, but otherwise the order stays constant. The conductor usually works towards one or more musical rows and then back to rounds. Call changes are often rung by inexperienced bands, but in Devon it is a speciality performed to a high standard.

METHODS

When ringing A method the order continually changes. A method is a systematic way of generating many different rows by repeating a simple sequence of changes. This is the dominant form of change ringing.

The simplest method is 'Plain Hunt'. Two changes keep alternating until the sequence returns to rounds (see *Fig. 7*). One change swaps all pairs and the other change swaps all pairs except the first and last bells. On four bells this pair of changes can be repeated four times, giving a sequence of eight rows. On six bells it repeats six times, giving twelve rows, and so on.

Plain Hunt can be extended to 'Plain Bob' if every time the treble (bell 1) returns to lead the first two bells are left fixed instead of first and last. This whole sequence then repeats several times before returning to rounds. On four bells it cycles three times giving a 'course' of twenty-four rows. With more bells it lasts longer. For example, on ten bells nine cycles of twenty rows give a course of 180 rows.

There are many more complex methods than this. Most are identified with a three-part name (a bit like plants) – a specific name, a family

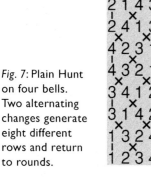

Fig. 7: Plain Hunt on four bells. Two alternating changes generate eight different rows and return to rounds.

name and a stage name. The specific name can be anything chosen by whoever first rings it in a performance. The family name defines its structure (how the changes fit together). The stage name is the number of bells changing. Examples include: Plain Bob Minor, Oxford Bob Triples, Primrose Surprise Major, Kent Treble Bob Royal, Avon Delight Maximus.

The number of potential methods is huge (see *Fig. 9*, overleaf). Around nineteen thousand have been named but many more are possible. Most ringers know a modest number of standard methods, and they ring them by learning the path of a bell as a pattern, not by memorising all the numbers.

COMPOSITIONS

Once started, a method will run its course because each ringer knows what to do without further instruction. A typical course lasts a few minutes, depending on the number of bells and type of method. Longer performances are achieved using 'calls'. A call is like a switch inserted at certain points in the method to direct the ringing along a new track, which it then follows until the next call. The conductor initiates calls at positions determined by the composition, which has to be learnt.

For a 'true' performance the composer must ensure that no row occurs more than once. That can require considerable ingenuity with some methods, especially for long performances. The quest for truth dates from the earliest days of change ringing in the seventeenth century and is so deeply respected that a peal discovered to be false after it has been rung is withdrawn from the records. Apart from record-length peals, which require an umpire to be recognised, ringing performances are not 'policed'. They are inherently public and the ringing community relies on the integrity of the conductor to report correctly what was rung.

One compositional feat took over three centuries to achieve. Stedman (named after its inventor Fabian Stedman) is a method with a simple, elegant structure amenable to compositions

1 2 3 4 5 6 (2)
2 1 4 3 6 5
2 4 1 6 3 5
4 2 6 1 5 3
4 6 2 5 1 3
6 4 5 2 3 1
6 5 4 3 2 1
5 6 3 4 1 2
5 3 6 1 4 2
3 5 1 6 2 4
3 1 5 2 6 4
1 3 2 5 4 6
1 3 5 2 6 4 (4)
3 1 2 5 4 6
3 2 1 4 5 6
2 3 4 1 6 5
2 4 3 6 1 5
4 2 6 3 5 1
4 6 2 5 3 1
6 4 5 2 1 3
6 5 4 1 2 3
5 6 1 4 3 2
5 1 6 3 4 2
1 5 3 6 2 4
1 5 6 3 4 2 (6)
5 1 3 6 2 4
5 3 1 2 6 4
3 5 2 1 4 6
3 2 5 4 1 6
2 3 4 5 6 1
2 4 3 6 5 1
4 2 6 3 1 5
4 6 2 1 3 5
6 4 1 2 5 3
6 1 4 5 2 3
1 6 5 4 3 2
1 6 4 5 2 3 (5)
6 1 5 4 3 2
6 5 1 3 4 2
5 6 3 1 2 4
5 3 6 2 1 4
3 5 2 6 4 1
3 2 5 4 6 1
2 3 4 5 1 6
2 4 3 1 5 6
4 2 1 3 6 5
4 1 2 6 3 5
1 4 6 2 5 3
1 4 2 6 3 5 (3)
4 1 6 2 5 3
4 6 1 5 2 3
6 4 5 1 3 2
6 5 4 3 1 2
5 6 3 4 2 1
5 3 6 2 4 1
3 5 2 6 1 4
3 2 5 1 6 4
2 3 1 5 4 6
2 1 3 4 5 6
1 2 4 3 6 5
1 2 3 4 5 6

Bells	Name	Number of rows	Time to ring	Bells	Name	Number of rows	Time to ring
3	Singles	6	12 sec	4	Minimus	24	¾ min
5	Doubles	120	4 min	6	Minor	720	25 min
7	Triples	5040	~3 hour	8	Major	40,320	Nearly a day
9	Caters	362,880	Over a week!	10	Royal	3,628,800	2½ months
11	Cinques	39,916,800	2½ years	12	Maximus	479,001,600	30 years
13	Sextuples	6,227,020,800	400 years	14	Fourteen	87,178,291,200	5,500 years
15	Septuples	1,307,674,368,000	83k years	16	Sixteen	20,922,789,888,000	1.3M years

Fig. 9: Stage names, number of different rows and approximate time to ring them all for different numbers of bells.

of enormous diversity. The question posed in the 1670s was whether it was possible to compose a true extent (5040) of Stedman Triples by using only what he called 'common bobs' as calls. (At a common bob the bell in fifths place remains and the other three pairs swap.) Stedman thought it ought to be possible but couldn't prove it. Successive generations of ringing mathematicians also tried and failed. In the 1950s the first computers were set to work on the problem. Finally in 1994 it was solved independently by different people.

CHANGE-RINGING MUSIC

The music of change ringing is unique, quite unlike 'tunes' played with other musical instruments. There are no fast or slow notes and no rapid repetitions of the same note. Every 'bar' (row) contains all the notes, and no two 'bars' are the same. Less obvious to the casual listener is the close relationship between successive rows caused by no bell moving more than one place, but that provides the essential balance between variety (to provide interest) and predictability (to maintain coherence) that we perceive as musical.

Two more features can add coherence to the sound of ringing. One is the almost universal custom of ringing 'open lead'

1 2 3 4 5 6 1 2 3 4 5 6   1 2 3 4 5 6 1 2 3 4 5 6

Handstroke   *Backstroke*   *Handstroke*   *Backstroke*

– with a pause every other row. The other is the custom of ringing odd-bell methods on an even number of bells with the tenor 'covering' – the lowest note sounding last every time. In musical terms every 'bar' ends comfortingly with the tonic. This custom is related to the fact that towers with more than five bells almost all have an even number.

Much of the ringing of a method consists of alternating high and low notes, but periodically a characteristic pattern emerges, typically a run of several notes up or down the scale, which then dissolves and appears again later. These familiar patterns – 'roll ups' – have a similar effect to that of a leitmotif in conventional music.

The ebb and flow between different types of pattern occurs in many methods and is most noticeable on eight or more bells. During periods of alternating high and low notes the brain may lock onto one or the other giving the effect of a 'low tune' working its way progressively through the high notes, or vice versa.

The structure of some methods makes them inherently more musical than others. Peal composers often go to great lengths to make their compositions more musical, for example, by including frequent roll ups. Such compositions may be harder to call but there are always conductors who rise to the challenge.

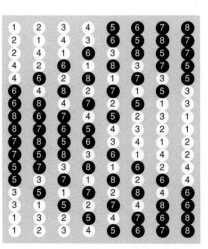

Fig. 10: The rhythm of open-lead ringing on six bells with a pause between each backstroke row and the following handstroke row.

Opposite bottom: Pealboard recording the first performance of a peal of Stedman Triples containing only 'common' (i.e. ordinary) bobs – a problem that took over three hundred years to solve.

Fig. 11: Plain Hunt on eight bells showing where the 'low tune' (bells 5, 6, 7, 8, shown black) moves progressively through the 'high tune' (bells 1, 2, 3, 4, shown white).

J. WARNER & SONS LONDON & AT WALTON ON THE NAZE ESSEX.

WITTON

J.WARNER & SONS LONDON

WITTON

EVOLUTION OF ENGLISH-STYLE RINGING

H OW DID ALL the complexity of change ringing evolve? To understand that we need to go back many centuries. English monasteries had large bells around the eighth century and later parish churches did too. Over time churches acquired more than one bell, and used different bells or combinations of bells to signal different services. By the late fifteenth century many churches had three or more, which set the stage for new uses.

In medieval times the Church was more closely integrated with the life of the community than it is today, and its bells were used for mass communication. They sounded curfews, announced markets and raised alarms (the latter echoed during the Second World War when the government banned ringing except to signal an invasion).

On occasions of public rejoicing several bells would be used together to make a joyous sound. They would be swung vigorously, which made the clappers strike both sides of the bell. Whereas a clerk could toll a single bell for services, this

Opposite: Eight ringers with their bells all set at handstroke, ready to ring, from a nineteenth-century catalogue by John Warner & Son.

Norman stone carving of a bellringer ('*campanarius*') at Stoke Dry, Northamptonshire.

more vigorous secular ringing would need several people, probably strong young men. They were paid, and there are records of payment from the mid fifteenth century. They presumably discovered that sounding bells in sequence was more pleasant than ringing randomly, and this would have required teamwork as well as physical effort. Hence ringing took on some of the characteristics of a sport.

EVOLUTION OF FULL-CIRCLE RINGING

Before about the fourteenth century bells in Britain were hung from a simple pivot and swung with a rope attached to a lever – they couldn't be swung anywhere near full circle. How and why full-circle ringing evolved is open to conjecture. We know it happened, and we know the stages through which the mechanism evolved to make it possible, but we can only guess at the motivation that led to such radical change in both the activity and the technology.

Example of a half wheel at Salthouse, Norfolk.

The key difference between swing chiming and full-circle ringing is control. At some point someone must have realised that they could change the timing more easily by swinging the bells much higher than when chiming. That would have set them on the path of innovation, even if at first they did not realise that ringing full circle would achieve so much control.

The first step was to add a quadrant to the lever to form a quarter wheel, thus letting the bell swing much higher, probably about half way up. Then came the half or three-quarter wheel,

which enabled the bell to swing almost full circle. That gave better control but there was still a major limitation: the ringer could only control alternate strokes, because at one end of the swing the rope didn't wrap around the wheel, and gave no purchase.

Bells hung for swing chiming with a simple lever at St Michael and All Angels, Hopton Wafers.

The critical step, made sometime in the sixteenth century, was to tie the rope with a cord (a 'garter') part way around the rim, or to peg it with a fillet, making it bend back on itself at the previously dead stroke. With the rope now winding both ways around the wheel the ringer had control of both strokes and could pause the bell near the balance at either stroke if needed. Modern terminology echoes this critical development – the point at which the rope passes through the wheel rim is called the 'garter hole' (or 'fillet hole').

Extending to a complete wheel was a relatively modest step. It made it easier to avoid 'throwing the bell over' by pulling too hard, but had relatively little other effect, since the rope never touches about a quarter of the wheel.

The final key innovation was to add a stay and slider, so that bells could be set at rest in the up position rather than having to raise and lower them before and after each piece of ringing.

Bells swinging full circle generate large forces – roughly four times each bell's weight downwards and twice its weight sideways – so bell frames had to be adapted to withstand these. By the fourteenth century bells were typically hung between a

Fig. 12: Evolution of the bell wheel. Extending from an arm to a quarter wheel to a half wheel extended the swing, and making the rope fold back on itself generated the two-stroke action.

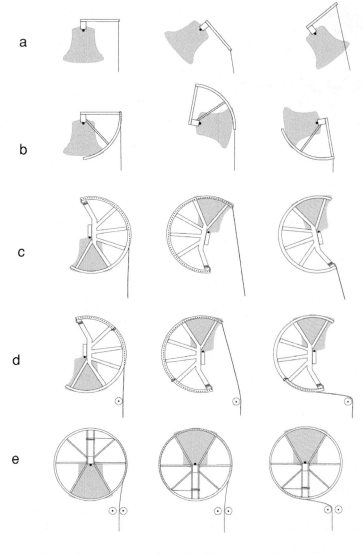

pair of wooden trusses, each with a king post and curved braces, all held together with wooden pegs. This evolved in stages to a frame of braced timber trusses held together by bolts. Modern installations normally use metal frames, with cast iron sides that carry the bells, joined together by lighter steel bars into a frame with the requisite number of bell pits. Most frames

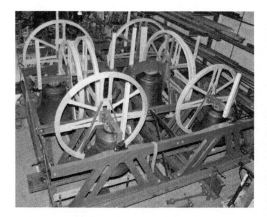

have some bells swinging at right angles to others in order to distribute the forces on the tower more evenly.

The frame, and the tower in which it sits, must be rigid enough to prevent significant movement, otherwise the bells can behave unpredictably and are difficult to ring. A sixteenth of an inch movement can have a noticeable effect on the way bells handle, and half an inch makes controlling them quite difficult. Heavy bells hung high in slender towers are the worst. A few such towers shake alarmingly during ringing, though the movement is less than it feels.

Above left: A typical modern bell frame assembled in the workshop of Whites of Appleton.

Above: Partial view of a medieval bell frame at Middleton, Warwickshire.

THE GROWTH OF CHANGE RINGING

Changing the order of the bells while ringing adds interest and variety, and it became easy with the development of the wheel. It is unclear whether ringers tried to do it before they rang full circle. If they did, it would have been much harder and might have provided the stimulus to develop the wheel. With bells swinging full circle it was straightforward, for when a pair of bells swap places one 'holds up' (pauses slightly) while the other 'cuts in'.

Ringers went on to develop systematic schemes for continually changing the order, probably in the late sixteenth or early seventeenth century – the phrase 'ring the changes' appeared in a sermon in 1614. By the 1660s many of the concepts of modern change ringing were already established, including much of the terminology.

Early change ringing used 'plain changes', where only one pair of bells swaps place at a time. These 'peals' had names like 'the six' (every possible order of three bells) and 'the twenty' (which was on five bells). Plain change ringing is simple in concept but would challenge modern ringers because individual bells move place infrequently, and knowing when to do so requires awareness of what several other bells are doing. The more dynamic 'cross peals', where several pairs can swap at once, were introduced during the seventeenth century. This style is now dominant though the term is no longer used.

The terminology used to describe ringing on different numbers of bells reflects the number of pairs that can swap at once. When ringing five bells only two pairs can do so – a 'double change' – hence the name 'Doubles'. On seven bells three pairs can swap at once, hence 'Triples'. On nine and eleven the names are 'Caters' and 'Cinques'. The terms (from the French '*quatre*' and '*cinque*') were used in gaming at the time ringing developed. Triples ringing was established by the mid 1600s, and since the first rings of ten were installed in the late 1600s it is reasonable to assume that Caters was being rung by then.

The status of change ringing as a sport in the late seventeenth century is clear from books such as *The School of Recreation*,

Metal plaque in St Andrew Undershaft in the City of London, commemorating ringer Fabian Stedman, who was buried there in November 1713.

or the Gentleman's Tutor: to those most ingenious exercises of hunting, racing, hawking, riding, cock-fighting, fowling, fishing, shooting, bowling, tennis, ringing and billiards, published in 1684. It describes ringing as: 'highly esteemed, for its excellent Harmony of Musick it affords the ear, for its Mathematical Invention delighting the Mind, and for the Violence of its Exercise bringing Health to the Body, causing it to transpire plentifully, and by Sweats dissipate and expel those Fuliginous thick Vapours, which Idleness, Effeminacy, and Delicacy subject men to'. The mental aspects are just as true today but the physical exercise on modern bells is far more gentle.

RINGING BOOKS

The first book devoted to change ringing was *Tintinnalogia* (1668). It was published by Fabian Stedman, an active London ringer, and it was a joint effort with Richard Duckworth who wrote much of the content. Stedman went on to write *Campanalogia* in 1677, which covered the developments of the intervening decade. It contained more cross peals and more peals from outside London.

Other authors followed where Stedman had led, and many of the early ones had related titles: *Campanalogia Improved* (1702), *Clavis Campanalogia or A Key to the Art of Ringing Dedicated to the Lovers of the Art* (1788), *The Campanalogia or Universal Instructor in the Art of Ringing* (1813–16).

RINGING SOCIETIES

In towns where more than one church had bells the ringers often had no allegiance to a particular tower and rang wherever they pleased, paying the sexton to let them in. They organised themselves into societies, with elaborate codes of conduct often in doggerel, some of which can be seen painted on boards in towers.

The earliest recorded ringing society, the Scholars of Cheapside, is known to have operated in London between

1603 and 1662. Other societies formed in the seventeenth century, many of which no longer exist. Among those that survive are: The Company of Ringers of the Blessed Virgin Mary of Lincoln (founded in 1612); Saffron Walden Society of Change Ringers (1623); Ancient Society of College Youths (1637); Society of Sherwood Youths (1672); Ancient Society of Painswick Youths (1686). Most of these still operate in a single town but the College Youths became one of two pre-eminent ringing societies with international membership, the

SOCIETY of COLLEGE YOUTHS
LONDON

Membership certificate of the Ancient Society of College Youths adapted for use as a dinner ticket in the eighteenth century.

other being the Society of Royal Cumberland Youths (1747), though 'Royal' was only added in the 1870s.

PEAL RINGING

The modern 'gold standard' performance is a peal – over five thousand different rows starting and ending with rounds, rung continuously without visual aids or external assistance – but in the seventeenth century a 'peal' was any ringing performance. The desire to avoid repetition was already present with ringers trying to find 'true peals', and especially what were known as 'complete peals', where every possible row was rung exactly once – an 'extent' in modern terms.

> If that to Ring you doe come here,
> you muſt Ring well with hand and eare.
> keep ſtroak of time and goe not out;
> or elſe you forfeit out of doubt.
> Our law is ſo concluded here;
> for every fault a jugg of beer,
> if that you Ring with Spurr or Hat;
> a jugg of beer muſt pay for that.
> If that you take a Rope in hand;
> theſe forfeits you muſt not withſtand.
> or if that you a Bell ovrthrow;
> it muſt coſt Six-pence ere you goe.
> If in this place you ſweare or curſe;
> Six-pence to pay pull out your purſe
> come pay the Clerk it is his fee;
> for one that ſwears ſhall not goe free.
> Theſe Laws are old, and are not new;
> therefore the Clerk muſt have his due.
> George Hariſon.

Ringers' rules dating from 1694 at Tong in Shropshire.

On four and five bells an extent only takes a few minutes to ring (twenty-four rows on four bells and 120 rows on five). Both were achieved by the mid seventeenth century. Ringing an extent on six bells (720 rows) takes nearly half an hour and on seven bells (5040 rows) around three hours.

The extent on seven bells proved to be a major challenge. Intellectually it was hard to devise a scheme to generate 5040 rows and prove they were all different. Physically and mentally, ringing for three hours without mistakes was arduous. Several unsuccessful attempts are known in the late seventeenth century and there must have been other unrecorded attempts. A peal was rung in London in 1690 but there is no written record of the performance. The first definitively recorded peal was on 2 May 1715 when the Norwich Scholars rang what they called Grandsire Bob Triples, which is now called Plain Bob Triples. It is a seven-bell method but they rang it in the

The pealboard at St Peter Mancroft, Norwich, showing the first recorded peal, rung in 1715.

normal way, on eight bells with the tenor 'covering' – ringing last each time.

Logically the next step would have been to ring the extent on eight (40,320 rows) but it would have taken around a day to ring, and for anyone to ring continuously for so long must have seemed beyond human capability (though a relay of ringers did manage to ring an extent of Plain Bob Major in twenty-seven hours in 1761).

Thus, as change ringing moved to higher numbers, the modern concept of a peal emerged, with a fixed minimum length on any number of bells. The required length is based on the extent on seven (5040) but since that exact length is impossible with many methods on eight or more, the minimum was set to a round number (5000) and the actual length is usually a little more. The first eight-bell peal was rung by the Union Scholars in December 1718 at St Dunstan in the East, London. They rang 5120 of what they called Union Bob Major (now called Oxford Treble Bob Major).

The Union Scholars had already rung the first nine-bell peal (Grandsire Caters in January 1717) and they went on to ring the first eleven-bell peal (Grandsire Cinques in January 1725), the first ten-bell peal (Plain Bob Royal in November 1725) and the first twelve-bell peal (Plain Bob Maximus in February 1726). Note the earlier dates for odd bell peals. Ringing with the tenor covering provides a stable framework for the music, and the heaviest bell doesn't have to be 'turned in', which is physically more demanding.

A fine eighteenth-century pealboard in the tower of St Mary the Great, Cambridge.

Standard length peals on fewer than seven bells require more than one extent, and these were first rung later than peals on higher numbers. The first six-bell peal was in March 1734/5 at St Mary de Crypt, Gloucester, and the first five-bell peal was in December 1756 at East Haddon, Northamptonshire.

Peal ringing grew. The high status of peals makes them a useful historical measure because there are far more complete records

ON MONDAY JAN.Y 21.st J788,
Was rung in this Tower,
A true and exquisite Peal,
consisting of 6600 Changes,
BOB ~ MAXIMUS,
In 5 Hours and 5 Minutes,
Without a false Change;
......BY......
The undermentioned
CAMBRIDGE YOUTHS.

Treble. I. SMITH   7th. T. JONES
2d. W. BLAND   8th. P. GOUDE
3d. R. LAUGHTON   9th. C. DAY
4th. J. LAWSON   10th. W. YOUNG
5th. J. COE   11th. J. HAZARD
6th. T. STEERS   Tenor. J. BOWTELL.

J. Willmott } Church
R. Wheeler } Wardens.   Bobs by C. Day

than for other ringing, much of which was unrecorded. In the twenty years following 1715 over a hundred more peals were rung across the country in places such as Canterbury, Ellesmere (Shropshire), Farnham (Surrey), Gloucester, Leicester, London, Reading, Wrexham and York. In the next twenty years over two hundred were rung, and by the end of the century over a thousand had been rung. But growth was erratic; for example, about sixty peals per year were rung around 1785, but only about twenty per year a couple of decades later.

Peal ringing really took off in the late nineteenth century, almost certainly as a result of the influence of the Belfry Reform movement (see the next chapter) and it has grown more or less continually ever since, apart from dips during the First and Second World Wars.

COMPETITION RINGING

Competition and rivalry were features of everyday life when ringing was developing, and ringers too became competitive. Ringing was one of the earliest organised group activities open to most of the population and much of the competitiveness was between bands of ringers. They took it seriously – for example, in the early 1600s rules of the Lincoln Cathedral ringers stipulated a substantial fine (twenty shillings) for 'ringing a match against the Company'.

In the eighteenth century dozens of ringing competitions were advertised in newspapers. The earliest known was at Carshalton in 1699. Sometimes a competition was used to 'open' a new ring of bells.

Ringing contests were often sponsored by local innkeepers, who also sponsored events such as pigeon shooting, cudgelling and cockfighting. The prizes were typically hats embroidered with gold or silver lace or tassels, one for each ringer and one for their 'umpire'. Sometimes a second prize was a set of gloves. The innkeepers provided the prizes, so they must have made their profit on the eating and drinking. Contestants had to eat 'the ordinary', a set meal that usually cost a shilling. Spectators must also have eaten and drunk well to make the events viable.

Very few towers had more than six bells so competitions were usually for five- or six-bell ringing, to ensure a good entry. The test was usually to raise the bells, ring a specified length of a set method and lower them again – between fifteen and thirty minutes' ringing for each team. In some parts of the country, notably the villages around Reading, competitions were for rounds ringing rather than methods. In one small town, Wokingham, four separate inns – the Ship, the Bush, the Six Bells and the Half Moon – all sponsored ringing contests in the late 1700s.

The Ship Inn, Wokingham, which sponsored many ringing competitions in the late 1700s.

Intense rivalry developed between some bands, quite apart from the public contests, especially in industrial towns in the early nineteenth century. This could become personal and bitter, and last for months or even years. A lot of money could be wagered on the results. For example, in a long-running rivalry between Oldham and Ashton the prize for a contest at Flixton in 1808 was forty guineas (over £200 in modern money). This was a far cry from the wholesome sport that ringing had once been.

THE DEMAND FOR BELLS

Associated with the growth of change ringing was an increasing demand for bells. One indicator is the number of bell foundries, which grew rapidly during the late sixteenth

Whitechapel Bell Foundry, England's oldest manufacturing business, dates from 1570 and has operated on its present site since 1738.

and seventeenth centuries, peaking at nearly sixty around 1700. The demand probably peaked too, but a later decline in the number of foundries was inevitable as better transport encouraged fewer, more efficient foundries. An increased demand for bells during the boom in Victorian church-building prior to the First World War didn't stop this process, and the number of foundries continued to drop. The closure of Gillett & Johnston's Croydon foundry in 1957 left only two UK bell founders: John Taylor in Loughborough and the Whitechapel Bell Foundry in London.

SPREAD BEYOND ENGLAND

Change ringing spread across England, across the British Isles and to the colonies. Ringing came to America in the mid eighteenth century (to Boston, Massachusetts, in 1744; to Dorchester, South Carolina, in 1753; to Philadelphia,

Pennsylvania, in 1754; and to Charleston, South Carolina, in 1764), but after the war of independence the British connection made it unpopular. Ringing came to Australia in the mid nineteenth century (to the Sydney churches of St Mary in 1843, St Benedict in 1849, St Philip in 1856, and to Hobart in Tasmania in 1846). Other commonwealth countries were somewhat later.

The dedication of a new ring of ten bells at Washington Cathedral in 1964 proved a turning point, and since then the number of ringing towers in USA has grown over five times (to 48). Over a similar period the number of ringing towers in Australia and South Africa more than doubled (to 59 and 10 respectively). But, despite this huge growth, 98 per cent of ringing towers are still in the British Isles.

Why didn't ringing spread to England's European trading partners? Different forms of full-circle ringing evolved in northern Italy but not change ringing. Carillons developed in the Netherlands around the same time as change ringing in England, and there are nearly three hundred of them in the Low Countries compared with fifteen in Britain. Perhaps the carillon met the community need for a 'joyful sound'.

2008 saw continental Europe's first English-style tower bells – a light ring of eight in 't Klokhuys, Dordrecht, Netherlands.

Fig. 13: Distribution of towers with three or more bells hung for English-style ringing: (a) England compared with other countries. (b) The British Isles excluding England. (c) Countries outside the British Isles.

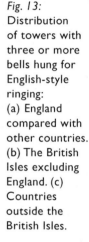

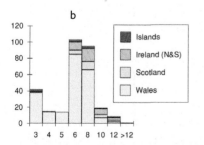

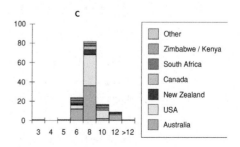

RINGING AND THE CHURCH

I N MODERN TIMES people outside the ringing community may see bellringing as 'just another thing that churches do' – a bit like hymn singing. But the previous chapter shows how English-style ringing – especially change ringing – evolved as an amalgam of sport and public entertainment. How did the Church fit into this story?

At first it didn't, other than to provide the bell tower. In medieval times religion had a strong influence, but church buildings were usually maintained by the Lord of the Manor and used for secular gatherings as well as services. Bells announced all manner of secular events – royal visits, military victories, local fairs, the curfew and much more, as well as calling people to church. It was from the more exuberant secular ringing that the art of ringing as we know it grew, quite separate from the liturgical chiming of bells. People rang on Sundays, just as with other sports, since it was the only day of the week many of them weren't working – but they didn't ring for services.

THE REFORMATION AND PURITANISM

In the sixteenth and seventeenth centuries the English Church went through great change with the Reformation and the rise of Puritanism. Worship was simplified, with anything thought to be superstitious or unnecessary swept away. The liturgical use of bells was greatly restricted, customs like ringing on All Hallows' Night to ward away evil spirits were banned and burial peals were replaced with tolling a single bell.

Opposite: The Right Reverend John Waine dedicating the Royal Jubilee Bells in St James Garlickhythe, now their permanent home after being rung at the head of the Queen's Diamond Jubilee river pageant in 2012.

The Crown had profited from the despoliation of the monasteries, and during the reign of Edward VI sought to confiscate valuables from other churches too. In 1552 a national inventory of church plate, bells and other valuables was ordered, but in fact few bells were seized. This suggests an awareness that although the post-Reformation Church had less need for bells, local communities still valued them – presumably for their secular use – and that removing them might arouse strong opposition and unrest.

The commissioners responsible for confiscations did bell historians a great service though, because their inventories record what they took and what they left, providing a valuable record of how many bells there were around 1550. Most churches had at least three bells and many, especially in towns, had four, five or even six.

The Church wanted to control the use of bells, and the incumbent had legal custody of them, but in practice he had limited say in their use. A country priest would not interfere with ringing done at the squire's bidding (or ordered by the civic authorities in towns). During the late sixteenth century many rings of bells were restored or augmented, which suggests that communities took pride in their bells and that there was plenty of (secular) ringing.

Sunday was a great day for sport, but the Puritans took a dim view of this and, as their influence grew, they sought to ban anything other than going to church on a Sunday. In 1595 Queen Elizabeth rejected a bill 'for better and more reverent observing of the Sabbath day' but in the same year a book on the doctrine of the Sabbath condemned ringing more than a single bell on Sundays. Another writer quotes a preacher in Suffolk saying that 'to ring more bells than one on the Lord's day to call the people to church was as great a sin as to do an act of murder'.

The Puritans believed that bells were popish, and they continued their hostility to ringing with increased vigour in the seventeenth century. The bells themselves were deemed to be sinful, especially if they had prayers inscribed on them. Inscriptions were filed off some bells after a parliamentary ordinance of 1643 for the removal of superstitious inscriptions from churches.

John Bunyan gives us an insight into the Puritan view of ringing. He had greatly enjoyed ringing in his youth during the 1640s but gave it up after joining a sect for which ringing, dancing and other such pastimes were sinful. He was still drawn to the tower to watch the ringing, but he felt that even this was sinful, and that a bell might strike him down or the tower fall on him in retribution.

John Bunyan rang in his youth but later joined a non-conformist sect which condemned ringing as sinful.

RESTORATION AND COEXISTENCE

After the Restoration many Puritan laws were repealed. Freed of restriction, as we saw in the previous chapter, ringing prospered and developed. Ringing was more or less independent of the Church and the two coexisted as they had before the Reformation. But the relationship changed, and by the early nineteenth century there was considerable tension.

One problem was drink. Ringing was thirsty work and ringers needed to quench their thirst. Beer was safer to drink than water, and ringers were often paid in beer for their ringing. Some kept beer in the tower, in a special jug or 'gotch' to sustain them when ringing throughout the day. Some of these jugs survive. The one at Beccles reputedly holds thirty-three pints – quite a weight when full – and the last person known to carry it full up the tower, around 1912, was a blacksmith named Robert Freestone. Inevitably there were drunken ringers, and it seems that they became more common as social conditions worsened during the Industrial Revolution.

Above: The Beccles ringers' gotch from 1827: 'When I am fill'd with Liquor strong / Each man drink once and then ding dong. / Drink not to much to Cloud your knobs / Lest you forget to make the Bobbs. / Gift of John Pattman, Beccles. Samuel Stringfellow Potter'

Above right: Cartoon depicting Robert Freestone carrying the gotch up Beccles tower.

The Church became more hostile to secular ringing. In 1765 the Rector of Beccles said it was not his business to control the ringing when asked to suspend it because someone near the tower was ill; however, a century later his successor adamantly refused to allow ringing for the revived Beccles races, despite public outcry. He locked the ringers out of the tower but they managed to 'break in' and ring as the community wished. No doubt he saw this as evidence of their 'unruliness'.

BELFRY REFORM

The Reverend Henry Thomas Ellacombe, born in 1790, took a different view. He saw a clear need for reform but respected the art of ringing. He wrote:

> Reared in a country parsonage, and close to a peal of eight
> bells, as musical and as well rung as any in the kingdom,
> it has been my lot from childhood to have seen much
> of the practices in a country belfry. They had better, I

RINGING OUT THE OLD YEAR IN THE BELFRY OF CRIPPLEGATE CHURCH.

A scene of early Victorian ringing and drinking at New Year in St Giles Church, Cripplegate, London.

grieve to say, be passed over in silence; for such things as I remember to have seen and heard would hardly be tolerated in a village ale-house ...

Ellacombe wanted to reform the ringers, not remove them. He managed to do this between 1817 and 1835 when he was incumbent at Bitton, Gloucestershire, which was a very rough area at the time. He encouraged the ringers to practise regularly during the week and to attend church services on Sunday, and he took control of their payment.

He still favoured chiming rather than ringing for services but he described the usual custom at the time as: '... miserable work ... the sexton and a boy ... jangle three or four bells'. He was a practical man who had studied engineering before ordination,

Right: Reverend Henry Thomas Ellacombe, a prime mover of the Belfry Reform movement.

Far right: An Ellacombe apparatus still in working order at Hurstpierpoint, Sussex. It allows one person to sound all the bells.

and he devised an apparatus (named after him) that enabled one person to produce a pleasing sound from all the bells.

Hammers beneath the bells were connected to a frame in the ringing room, and they could be brought into position close to the bells by tensioning the ropes in the frame. Each bell could then be sounded by drawing out its respective rope a few inches. The resulting sound is less rich than full-circle ringing but is pleasing when done well. It is even possible to play tunes – though having only six or eight notes severely limits the repertoire.

Around the same time the Church underwent major change. The 'Oxford Movement', inspired by a group of young High Churchmen wishing to restore an element of Catholicism, swept away many old practices and triggered much change and restoration in churches. The ringers, operating independently, were largely untouched by this but not for long. Inspired by Ellacombe, other clerics began to follow his example and 'Belfry Reform' took hold. The aim was to bring ringers into line in return for improving their lot. A leading light was Reverend Woolmore Wigram (1831–1907).

He was an active ringer, though by all accounts not a very good one. He published thoughts on reform while an undergraduate at Cambridge and put them into practice as Rector of St Andrew's Hertford in the 1870s. He encouraged ringing

Canon Woolmore Wigram, a leading proponent of Belfry Reform.

for service, thus recognising ringers as church workers. He allowed ringing for public events but only those for which it would be equally appropriate to open the church and 'employ the organ and choir without irreverence'.

The reformers created new societies where ringers could join together for support and advancement. Ellacombe helped found the first of these, the Guild of Devonshire Ringers, in 1874, and by 1900 they covered much of the country. The societies often hired instructors to visit towers, help train ringers and report progress. Non-ringing clergy and local gentry often became honorary members, paying a higher subscription than ringers. University ringing societies were founded in the 1870s (in Oxford in 1872 and in Cambridge in 1879) so that men destined for the clergy could experience ringing, which would help them later to drive reform in their parishes.

The Guild of Devonshire Ringers was the first society set up by the Belfry Reformers. Its membership certificate clearly shows the influence of ecclesiastical architecture.

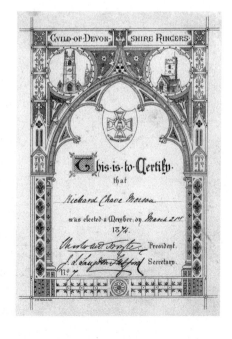

This picture of Reverend Francis Edward Robinson, founder and first Master of the Oxford Diocesan Guild of Church Bell Ringers, hangs in many towers within the diocese.

Change ringing was at the heart of Belfry Reform, which might seem odd since it evolved as a secular sport and had no connection with liturgical music. But many of the reforming clergy were ringers who knew the intellectual stimulation it provided and no doubt they felt that engagement of the mind as well as the body would encourage other worthy habits.

POST REFORM

The reform did far more than tame unruly ringers, not that they were all unruly. With the Church's encouragement, ringing flourished – both service ringing and the wider art, which still had a secular flavour. Many leading ringers were clergy. The first person to ring a thousand peals was Reverend Francis Edward Robinson in 1905, and he went on to ring over 1,250, the last shortly before he died, aged seventy-seven. Clergy made up 20 per cent of the members of the Central Council of Church Bell Ringers when it was founded in 1891, but after the 1920s their numbers declined – to around 1 per cent in modern times.

After the First World War disillusionment caused a decline in organised religion and ringing suffered because recruits were mainly drawn from the Church. But ringing revived after the Second World War, and the recruitment of ringers from outside the Church as well as inside became more common.

One adverse effect of the Victorian reforms was to curtail secular ringing for the community, whether by intent or neglect. This seriously weakened the relationship between ringers and the wider community outside the Church.

THE MODERN ERA

Ringers and the Church today have a symbiotic relationship. Ringers provide a service that enhances the life of the Church community and the Church provides ringers with a natural home and bells to ring. Some ringers are committed Christians for whom ringing is an act of worship, some are non-Christians happy to ring for the Church in return for the pleasure of ringing, and many others come somewhere in between. Most ringers see themselves as a part, albeit a semi-detached part, of the wider parish community.

Philip Aspinal, Archbishop of Brisbane, leaves his mitre, robes and crook behind to bless the refurbished bells at St Paul, Maryborough, Queensland. His microphone is linked to the church below.

Most modern clergy recognise ringing as a distinct activity in its own right (like organ playing, choral singing or flower arranging) which adds an extra dimension and richness to parish life. They support their ringers and encourage them to play an active role outside the tower, but they recognise that

The Italianate church at Saltaire was built by Sir Titus Salt for his mill workers. It had its first ring of change-ringing bells in 1870 and is one of only two United Reform churches that have a ring of bells.

not all ringers will wish to do so. They welcome the sound of ringing coming from their towers since it reminds the community, especially people who never venture inside, that the Church is alive.

One event where a parish and the wider ringing community come together is the dedication of a ring of bells. Funding for such projects normally comes from all sectors of the community, whose representatives, along with former ringers and ringers from elsewhere, swell the local congregation. The dedication is often performed by handing a token rope to the bishop who pronounces a blessing and hands it back for the bells to be rung. Sometimes bells are blessed in the church before being hung in the tower (see page 34). On at least one occasion a bishop went up among the bells to bless them in situ (see page 43).

Most bells are still in Anglican churches but some are in churches of other denominations. Prior to the Roman Catholic Relief Act of 1829, Catholic churches in England were banned from having bells, but from the mid nineteenth century onwards a few installed rings of bells. There are currently around thirty (0.5 per cent of the UK total). Other denominations have fewer rings of bells (currently just over 0.1 per cent of the UK total).

A church warden giving a hand during a bell restoration project.

MODERN RINGING

A TYPICAL MODERN ringer's routine includes ringing for Sunday services and a weekly practice. Some ring for services at several towers, and some attend more than one practice. Many ring for weddings, which is paid unlike almost all other ringing. Active ringers do far more than this. Many bands organise outings, travelling between towers to ring on different bells and see different places. Ringing societies run events where ringers from different bands ring together.

Training is a continual feature of ringing life, with trainees receiving many hours of individual tuition before they are ready to join in the main practice, and then hours of further support to help them develop their skills. Some towers act as 'ringing centres', devoted to training and equipped with modern teaching aids.

Opposite: Modern ringers in a historic setting – continuing a centuries-old tradition.

The teaching room at Worcester Cathedral, showing eight dumbbells.

Change ringing in hand – the author and three others performing at an annual ringers' dinner.

Many ringers enjoy ringing changes on handbells as well as tower bells, but this is rarely seen in public, unlike handbell tune ringing. It is easier to control the timing of a handbell than a tower bell, but since the ringers have a bell in each hand the mental task of working out when to strike them is much greater.

PERFORMANCES

For nearly all general ringing, practices and services, there are more ringers present than bells, with ringers taking turns to ring in different 'touches' lasting five to ten minutes each. For longer performances, the band is pre-arranged with one ringer per bell, and participants sometimes come from far and wide. The 'gold standard' performance is a peal, which typically takes around three hours (less on light bells, more on heavy bells). Around five thousand peals are rung each year of which about 15 per cent are on handbells. Some ringers never ring a peal and many just ring a few for special occasions, but some ring them regularly. Each year about three thousand ringers ring at least one peal. About a third ring only one, but the leading peal ringer often rings over two hundred.

Reverend Francis Edward Robinson was the first person to ring a thousand peals in 1905, but by 1955 twenty had done so and by 2015 over 490 had, of whom eighteen had rung over four thousand, four over five thousand and one over six thousand.

Quarter peals became popular in the twentieth century and are rung more often (around thirteen thousand per year) than peals, with well over a quarter of ringers taking part.

'Date touches', whose length matches the year when they are rung, are less common but are becoming more popular. There are no stock compositions available as there are for peals and quarters, so new ones are needed each year. Date touches can be 'backdated' to mark historic events; for example, a 1616 might be rung in 2016 to mark the 400th anniversary of Shakespeare's death.

Performances for sombre occasions like Remembrance or a funeral are often rung 'half muffled'. Each clapper has a leather pad on one side making alternate strokes loud and soft, which gives a dignified sound. In recent years it has become more common to ring open to celebrate someone's life rather than half muffled to mourn their death.

One of a pair of cast bronze striking competition trophies, each depicting a bell with two ringers inset (Sonning Deanery Branch of Oxford Diocesan Guild).

COMPETITIONS

Modern ringing competitions are organised by ringers – not innkeepers, as in the eighteenth century – with no valuable prizes. Most are on six bells but some are on eight or more.

The Taylor Trophy for the National Twelve Bell Contest.

The team from Hertfordshire that won the first ever Ringing World National Youth Contest in 2011.

There are several regional contests and two national ones. Around twenty teams enter the National Twelve Bell contest. Eliminators are in March and the final in June is attended by up to eight hundred ringers who consume a couple of thousand pints of beer and eat a prodigious amount of food. It is followed live on the Internet by hundreds of ringers worldwide. The Ringing World National Youth Contest attracts teams of ringers aged under nineteen from across the country.

PUSHING BOUNDARIES

There is a lot more ringing on higher numbers than there was in the mid-twentieth century. Between 1960 and 2015 the number of twelve bell towers more than doubled, with nearly 50 per cent more tens. There are also two rings of fourteen (Winchester and Osset) and three of sixteen (Birmingham, Dublin and Perth in Western Australia).

The maximum handbells rung in a peal, which stood at twelve since 1816, increased through fourteen (in 1922) to twenty-two (in 1978). In the Methodist Hall, Westminster, in

The 1973 reunion of the band that rang the extent of Plain Bob Major at Loughborough in 1963 – 40,320 changes in just under eighteen hours: (back row) Paul Taylor (founder), John Eisel, John Robinson, Brian Harris, Bob Smith, Peter Staniforth (umpire); (front row) Brian Woodruffe, John Jelley, Neil Bennett, Rick Shallcross.

2011 twelve ringers with twenty-four bells rang a special touch (short performance) of a hundred changes to an audience of around a thousand to mark *The Ringing World* centenary.

In 1963 eight ringers, ringing continuously for just under eighteen hours, did what *Tintinnalogia* in 1668 declared to be 'altogether impossible' by ringing the extent on eight bells – 40,320 Plain Bob Major at the Loughborough Foundry bell tower. By the end of 2014 this feat had not been repeated on tower bells, but in 2007 three ringers rang continuously for just over twenty-four hours in a peal of 72,000 Treble Dodging Minor on handbells.

On the fringes of ringing there have been some other feats including ringing two tower bells in a peal, ringing four handbells in a peal, and ringing peals blindfolded (a challenge for sighted ringers, who rely on visual cues – though blind ringers obviously don't). A few people have performed the ultimate mental feat – ringing all the bells, not conventionally but by 'tapping' handbells

The band that in 2007 rang a peal of 72,000 changes on handbells, taking over twenty-four hours: Philip Earis, Andrew Tibbetts, David Pipe.

hung in a frame with a small hammer. Elijah Roberts tapped several peals including 19,440 Kent Treble Bob Maximus in 13 hours and 43 minutes in 1837.

TECHNOLOGY

Ringing is a centuries-old tradition but ringers can be quick to use modern technology. Computers have been used to aid composition since the 1950s when the Ferranti Mk I machine at Manchester University ran a program trying to solve a ringing problem. Ringing simulators appeared in the late 1970s. They enable a trainee to ring a bell that feels and sounds as normal, but without needing ringers for the other bells, whose sound (ringing perfectly) is made by the simulator. Ringers also use simulator software running on personal devices to practise the mental skills of ringing methods – by pressing keys when their 'bell' should strike.

A ringer practising individually using a ringing simulator.

The National Twelve Bell contest developed a 'strikeometer' to help the judges with the difficult task of assessing the quality of near perfect ringing. Using a high-quality audio feed, it analyses the timing of each blow to give an overall measure of each team's accuracy. This technology should eventually filter down for use as a routine training aid.

Modern ringers are well served with online databases of ringing performances. The Felstead database lists the date, place and method of all known peals – Canon K. W. H. Felstead started it as a card index in the 1950s. PealBase contains details, including ringers and footnotes, of peals since 1950. Campanophile and BellBoard allow ringers to submit their performance details online and shows full details of peals, quarter peals and other performances since 2005.

SECULAR TOWERS

A few rings have always been in civic buildings – Morpeth Clock Tower (1706), Berwick-upon-Tweed Town Hall (1754) and Manchester Town

Hall (1877). In modern times the number of bells not in active churches is increasing. Between 1970 and 2010, 10 per cent of Anglican churches were made redundant, a trend likely to continue. Nearly eighty former churches with bells are now community centres or museums. There are also several private rings. The earliest extant is the twelve at Quex Park, Birchington, Kent, installed in 1819 by the eccentric John Powell Powell. One of the most prolific in terms of peal ringing is Loughborough Bell Foundry tower (dating from 1899), originally an eight and now a twelve. A more recent private ring is the twelve at the Ringing Centre, Tulloch, Highland (2013).

The bell tower, part of the Grade II*-listed building at Taylor's Loughborough Bell Foundry, held eight bells when built in 1899 and now houses a ring of twelve.

Perhaps the most spectacular secular tower architecturally is the Bell Tower in Perth, Western Australia. Twelve of its ring of sixteen bells were cast in the 1700s and rung at St Martin in the Fields, London, until 1988.

A few ringers have installed 'mini-rings' in houses or outbuildings. There is no agreed definition of 'mini' but the heaviest has a tenor just over two hundredweight, and most weigh much less, some only a few pounds. Portable mini-rings have proved valuable to show ringing in action to the public. Non-ringers can 'have a go' since light bells are safe with novices.

The Bell Tower, Perth, Western Australia, houses a ring of sixteen bells and a carillon. It is a major tourist attraction with public ringing performances most days.

THE RINGING COMMUNITY

Estimates suggest there are around forty thousand active ringers. Most belong to one or more of around seventy territorial ringing societies. There are also over twenty university societies (for alumni, not just students) as well as societies based on a profession or common interest. There are two premier societies: the Society of Royal Cumberland Youths and the Ancient Society of College Youths.

The Central Council of Church Bell Ringers represents ringers worldwide. Its work covers training and publications; advice on bell installation, maintenance and restoration; technical aspects of change ringing and performance records; and public relations, ringing trends and regulatory aspects. The Association of Ringing Teachers (founded in 2012) promotes high standards of teaching.

The ringing fraternity is like a large extended family. A ringer walking unannounced into almost any tower in the

Above left: Pealboard recording the first peal rung at The Black Bull Inn, Frosterley, County Durham, in 2005.

Above: The Charmborough Ring during a demonstration to interested members of the public in Oxford in 2013.

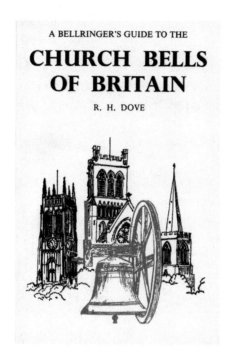

A BELLRINGER'S GUIDE TO THE

CHURCH BELLS OF BRITAIN

R. H. DOVE

Dove's Guide is an invaluable directory of ringing towers in Britain and abroad.

world will be made welcome and invited to ring. Visiting is facilitated by *Dove's Guide*, which has comprehensive information on over six thousand towers worldwide. It was first published by Ronald Hammerton Dove in 1950 and now has an online version.

The demography of ringers changed in the twentieth century. For example, the leaders of one tower between 1880 and 1980 were, by trade, farmer, postman, blacksmith, gardener and plumber, but the six since 1980 were all professionals: engineers, accountants or scientists. A 2011 survey of university ringers showed that three quarters studied maths, science or engineering. The age profile also changed, partly reflecting trends in the general population. Many of the post-war generation who learnt in their teens remained active for longer, and more ringers started later in life, while career pressures meant that fewer rang in their twenties and thirties. This all skewed the age distribution.

THE PUBLIC FACE OF RINGING

The most spectacular public performance of change ringing was in June 2012 at the head of the Thames river pageant for Queen Elizabeth II's Diamond Jubilee. It was seen by a million on the riverbank and millions more on TV. The bells now hang in St James Garlickhythe, London.

Some towers are tourist attractions, with exhibitions about ringing. One is at Inveraray, on the shore of Loch Fyne in Argyll. The tower was built in memory of members of Clan Campbell killed in the First World War, and contains the world's second heaviest ring of ten, with a tenor over two tons.

Ringing periodically features in fiction, most famously in *The Nine Tailors* by Dorothy L. Sayers and more recently in the UK radio soap opera *The Archers*. The TV series *Midsomer Murders* featured bellringing in the episode *Ring Out Your Dead*. The six actors playing the ringers all learnt to handle a bell – one so well that he was invited to join in ringing for a wedding.

While the sound of ringing is very public, the action is mostly hidden, which is a pity since it is a fascinating activity as well as being part of our cultural heritage. You may be able to see ringing in action locally by contacting your local tower and referring to the Places to Visit.

The Royal Jubilee bells aboard the *Ursula Katherine* near Hungerford Bridge on the Thames in London.

RINGING TERMINOLOGY

Backstroke (in full-circle ringing) when the bell is mouth up with the ringer reaching up to hold the tail end (opposite to handstroke)

Bob call that alters the course of an odd number of bells (normally three)

Call (n) Bob or single; (v) take charge of a piece of ringing by giving the commands

Call changes (n) periodically calling a pair of bells to swap positions

Campanology bellringing (mainly used by non-ringers)

Carillon twenty-three or more stationary bells rung from a clavier

Caters type of method with nine working bells

Change transformation between one row and the next

Change ringing ringing where the bells strike in a continually changing order

Cinques type of method with eleven working bells

Conductor person in charge of a ringing performance who calls the calls

Course natural length of a change-ringing method (plain course)

Dodge reverse step in change ringing that causes a pair of adjacent bells to swap places three times before continuing

Doubles type of method with five working bells

Down when a bell is hanging mouth downwards, safe but not ready for ringing

Exercise (the) collective term for ringing and the ringing community (widely used by ringers)

Extent performance or composition containing every possible row

False performance or composition in which one or more rows is repeated

Garter hole hole in wheel rim through which the rope passes and is attached

Gotch large jug for containing beer in the tower (historic)

Grandsire a basic, widely rung, odd-bell method – one of the earliest

Gudgeon metal pin on each end of the headstock, fitted with a bearing

Half muffled ringing with a leather pad on one side of each clapper giving alternate loud and soft rows

Handstroke (in full-circle ringing) when the bell is mouth up with the ringer reaching up to hold the sally (opposite to backstroke)

Headstock metal or timber beam carrying bell, wheel, gudgeons and stay

Hunt in change ringing, move continually from first to last place and back

Lead (1) position of the first bell in a row; (2) subdivision of a course during which the hunt bell (treble) makes one cycle from leading back to leading

Major type of method with eight working bells

Maximus type of method with twelve working bells

Method named sequence of changes that determines the progression of ringing

Minimus type of method with four working bells

Minor type of method with six working bells

Inveraray bell tower was built as a war memorial and houses the world's second heaviest ring of ten bells. It dominates the landscape and has become a major tourist attraction.

Muffled alternative term for half muffled

Peal performance with at least 5040 changes (Triples and below) or 5000 changes (Major and above)

Plain Bob a basic method that can be rung on any number of bells

Quarter peal performance with at least 1260 changes (Triples and below) or 1250 (Major and above)

Queens popular row in call changes in which odd bells are followed by even bells, e.g. 135246, 13572468

Ring collective name for bells in a tower, e.g. a ring of eight

Ringing up swinging a bell from the down position progressively higher until it can be set in the up position

Ropesight the skill of being able to see by looking at the moving ropes how one's own bell relates to what the others are doing during change ringing

Rounds bells rung down the scale

Row sequence in which each bell strikes exactly once

Royal type of method with ten working bells

Sally thick tufted woollen part of bell rope for a ringer to grip at handstroke

Set a bell swing it just past the balance point, stopping it and resting it against the stay

Single call that alters the course of an even number of bells (normally two)

Stand command to end the ringing by setting all bells

Stay wooden post attached to the headstock against which the bell can be rested mouth up (and weak enough to break before any other component if the bell is mishandled)

Stedman an early, much-loved method, invented by Fabian Stedman, with an elegant structure which allows for compositions of enormous diversity

Striking the rhythmic quality of ringing; perfect striking has equal intervals between each successive sound

Surprise a class of complex methods popular with experienced ringers

Tail end lower end of the rope, normally doubled up to provide a better grip

Tenor lowest-toned bell in a ring of bells (normally the heaviest)

Tied bell a bell with its clapper fixed to prevent it striking; used with a simulator or to teach basic handling

Touch change ringing performance

Treble highest-toned bell in a ring of bells (normally the lightest)

Triples type of method with seven working bells

True a composition in which no row is repeated

Up when a bell is mouth up, set just beyond the balance point ready for ringing

Whole-pull complete cycle including both handstroke and backstroke

FURTHER READING

Cubitt, Maureen. *The Bells Told: The Story of Ringers and Ringing at St Peter Mancroft, Norwich.* Jigsaw Design & Publishing, 2014.

Eisel, John (Compiler). *Order and Disorder in the early Nineteenth Century: Newspaper extracts about Church Bells and Bellringing.* Friends of CCCBR Library, 2013.

Elphick, George. *The Craft of the Bellfounder.* Phillimore, 1988.

Frith, Anne, Osborne, Vivienne, Smith, Dorothy. *Hark to the Bells: A History of Beccles as Told by the Bells and their Ringers.* A. Deed Frith, 2011.

Grave, Karl. *Yorkshire Tails: The Story of Bingley Bells and Ringers.* The Whiting Society of Ringers, 2009.

Harrison, John. *Living Heritage: 300 Years of Bells, Ringing and Ringers at All Saints, Wokingham.* John Harrison, 2009.

Jennings, Trevor. *Bellfounding*. Shire, 1988.

Sanderson, Jean (Editor), Cook, William T., Eisel, John C. *Change Ringing: The History of an English Art: Volume 1, Its Development up to 1699*. The Central Council of Church Bell Ringers, 1987.

Sanderson, Jean (Editor), Eisel, John C., Wratten, Cyril A. *Change Ringing: The History of an English Art: Volume 2, The Eighteenth Century and Overview*. The Central Council of Church Bell Ringers, 1992.

Sanderson, Jean (Editor), Cook, William T., Wratten, Cyril A. *Change Ringing: The History of an English Art: Volume 3, The Eighteenth Century a Regional Survey*. The Central Council of Church Bell Ringers, 1994.

Wratten, Cyril (Compiler), Eisel, John (Editor). *Order and Disorder in the Eighteenth Century: Newspaper Extracts About Church Bells and Bellringing*. Friends of CCCBR Library, 2010.

USEFUL WEBSITES

Association of Ringing Teachers: www.ringingteachers.co.uk

BellBoard: www.bb.ringingworld.co.uk (details of peals and quarter peals in recent years)

Campanophile: www.campanophile.co.uk (news and details of peals and quarter peals in recent years)

Central Council of Church Bell Ringers: www.cccbr.org.uk (represents English-style bell ringers worldwide)

Central Council of Church Bell Ringers bibliography: www.cccbr.org.uk/bibliography (current and former ringing publications grouped by topic)

Change Ringing Resources: www.ringing.info (eclectic collection of ringing-related links)

The Changeringing Wiki: www.wiki.changeringing.co.uk (Wiki devoted to ringing-related topics)

Discover Bell Ringing: www.bellringing.org (useful introductory website)

Dove's Guide for Church Bell Ringers: www.dove.cccbr.org. uk (details of towers with bells hung for ringing)

Felstead Database: www.felstead.org.uk (database of all known peals)

Keltek Trust: www.keltektrust.org.uk (charitable body for conservation and re-use of bells)

Mini-ring Directory: www.campaniles.co.uk/directory.html (description of all known mini-rings)

Ringing Glossary: www.johnharrison.me.uk/ringing/glossary (definition of 900 ringing-related terms)

The Ringing World: www.ringingworld.co.uk (weekly journal for ringers, established in 1911)

PLACES TO VISIT

Your local tower – ringers at most towers are happy to welcome visitors and show them what ringing is about. Details are usually near the tower or on their website. You can find the location of ringing towers using the Dove database (see above).

Other places to visit are as follows:

John Taylor & Co., The Bellfoundry (& Museum), Freehold Street, Loughborough, Leicestershire LE11 1AR. Telephone: 01509 212241. Website: www.taylorbells.co.uk

Whitechapel Bell Foundry, 32/34 Whitechapel Road, London E1 1DY. Telephone: 020 7247 2599. Website: www.whitechapelbellfoundry.co.uk

INDEX